Zen Moments

VENERABLE MASTER MIAO TSAN

bright sky press
HOUSTON, TEXAS

bright sky press
HOUSTON, TEXAS

2365 Rice Boulevard, Suite 202,
Houston, Texas 77005

www.brightskypress.com

Library of Congress Cataloging-in-Publication Data
on file with publisher.

10 9 8 7 6 5 4 3 2 1

ISBN 978-1-939055-43-9

Editorial Direction, Lucy Chambers
Design, Elena Reznikova
Printed in Canada through Friesens

Translations of Calligraphy by Chapter:

Chapter 1
Truth

Chapter 2
One Composite

Chapter 3
Right Understanding

Chapter 4
The Creator

Chapter 5
Karma

Chapter 6
Peace

Chapter 7
Purification

Chapter 8
Path of Light

Chapter 9
Enlightenment

Chapter 10
Joyful Mind

Zen Moments

ACKNOWLEDGEMENTS

A book is a collaboration of talent, and this one has benefited from the efforts of many dedicated individuals. I would like to acknowledge the following people for their support of *Zen Moments*.

Jay Gao compiled the text and quotations drawn from previously published books and organized them according to the theme of each chapter.

Ludmila Golovine dedicated her boundless energy to the creative process of this book. Through her whole-hearted commitment and generous support, this beautiful collection of 108 meditations in words and art has finally come into being in the world.

At MasterWord Services, Inc., Adrianne Poyet-Smith, who originally conceived of the idea for this project, made many contributions that helped the book to evolve to its present form. Elena Reznikova created 108 watercolor illustrations of a blossoming lotus that symbolize the unfolding of the authentic Self. She and David Vidrí collaborated on layout design. Alex Zinchenko managed the translation coordination and many project-related logistics.

Jui-Min (Richard) Su offered valuable insights and counsel in finalizing the content, design, and many other aspects of this project.

Special thanks to Lucy Chambers, who edited and finalized the manuscript and has seen the project through to its printing and final publication.

Shih, Miao Tsan
Fall 2015

TABLE OF CONTENTS

Walk With Me ix

Chapter 1 Truth 1

Chapter 2 Attachment 25

Chapter 3 Impermanence 49

Chapter 4 Phenomena 73

Chapter 5 Karma 97

Chapter 6 A Peaceful Mind 121

Chapter 7 Purity 145

Chapter 8 Dedication 169

Chapter 9 Awakening 193

Chapter 10 Practice 217

WALK WITH ME

Whether you have walked the Zen path for years or are just beginning to explore, welcome. In the following pages, I have collected 108 thoughts, as many as there are beads on a mala, for you to contemplate. Read one a day, read them sequentially, read them in any order or manner that strikes you. As you read and revisit these pearls, it is my hope that you will understand that the joy is in the journey, the peace in the practice. When you have mastered your mind, you can master your life.

千葉蓮臺千世界
有情心蓮有情開
毗盧頂上立處香
豈是淨土特意栽

Thousand-petaled lotus, thousand worlds

Sentient Mind, blossoming lotus

Atop the Crown of Vairocana, ambrosia permeates

Never a Pureland borne of deliberate intent

實相

1 TRUTH

Every religion has its own philosophy and customs, but the common goal is to understand the timeless truth that governs the working of the universe, from the cosmic level to our individual lives. Regardless of what we try to accomplish as human beings — health, successful careers, meaningful relationships, joy for ourselves, or peace for humanity as a whole — the understanding of the truth is the only way to guarantee fulfillment in life. Only the truth can lead us from darkness and confusion to the end of suffering and eternal happiness.

We must accept reality as it is,

not as we have chosen to define it.

The understanding and acceptance of reality

marks the true beginning of change.

The universal truth is the law of creation

under which life is formed,

and each of us has the innate ability

to create our own life phenomena.

The key to the mastery of our destiny is to learn how to properly shape our view toward life. Everyone has a point of view, but often such views are opinions that are not in accordance with the truth.

Do not see life as good or bad,

as if it were only black and white.

The truth is that good and bad coexist

within the confines of life.

Keep the mind open and flexible in every moment. If you cannot face life's reality but instead remain in a state of delusion, true freedom will not be yours.

Your thoughts, character, body, environment,

and relationships, whether good or bad,

are results created by your mind.

There is no truth outside the Mind.

Right now your mind is reflecting the relationships it creates. If these relationships are not desirable, you must begin to function from a different mental framework in order to achieve a different result.

The Mind is like a sponge:

when it is soaked with water, even when immersed in the ocean of knowledge, it won't absorb much more, except on the very surface layer.

If your thinking is not opened up, new ideas cannot be received and utilized.

Reverence for the truth is

the only wise form of reverence.

The mind frame of a child is not yet mature,

so we must nurture it and guide it.

In the grand universe, we humans are still children,

needing to find our way. We should not cling

too tightly to what we believe.

A joyful mind glows

with beautiful spring blossoms.

An angry mind burns out

winter mountain chrysanthemums.

A sorrowful mind falls low from its great height

like a summer waterfall.

A happy mind shines

like an autumn moon over the dike.

一合相

如来

2 ATTACHMENT

Human beings create suffering because we use our habitual thoughts to define reality, and in the process we distort it. Just as the boat used to cross a river should be abandoned upon arrival at the shore, thoughts are only tools for better living. They do not define the essence of who we are. We can, however, elevate our lives by recognizing our attachment to habitual thoughts and letting them go. Once we clear away the old thinking and beliefs, we create space for fresh ideas and inspirations that will lead to better actions and results. There is no need for us to cling to old tools that no longer serve a purpose.

Letting go is a gift unlike any other,

because it is a gift you give to yourself.

In order to change the world,

you must first change your mind.

To move from chaos toward freedom, the first thing we have to do is to correct how we think and get rid of our attachment to old, erroneous ideas.

People see the world through the lenses of their habits; when confronted with challenges, they hope the world will change to suit their habits.

They miss the point that it is they themselves who need to change.

If we, as the creator of the world, remain the same, how can the world change?

The mind is infinite in its function,

but its capacity has become restricted by habit.

Whether you are spiritual or not, whether or not you are wealthy or of respectable status, suffering and dissatisfaction are the unavoidable experience of all human beings. Suffering is caused by attachments and habitual tendencies that manifest as obstacles in your physical body and environment.

As our human minds continuously and unconsciously give rise to mind functioning, certain patterns emerge. These patterns channel our thinking in a particular, fixed direction.

Every stressful experience in our lives emerges from a mental door that we unconsciously but repeatedly open.

A new idea is like a stranger;

even if you had a good chat with him and developed

a positive feeling, it will still take a while until you

feel comfortable enough to invite him home.

The key to learning is to transform new

ideas into applicable conviction.

Spiritual growth is the process of opening up the self instead of externally accumulating knowledge.

Freedom from attachment is letting go;

doing our best is the act of taking up, or engaging.

In the journey of life, we must practice both

letting go and taking up.

正知見

妙柔

3 IMPERMANENCE

Everything that is created is destined for destruction. The atoms and cells in our body change constantly, relationships and business situations shift, and feelings of elation and depression come and go. Similarly, ideas and beliefs appear and disappear from moment to moment. We must recognize that nothing in this world of form can be grasped, because the nature of form is impermanence. A life built on the pursuit of form is filled with pain and disappointment. We must recognize the nature of existence and realize that behind the impermanent world of form lies our true refuge: the formless, eternal, boundless, pure Mind.

We must strive for higher existence

in each moment.

Early summer light floats and radiates;

Lazy southern breeze slows down time.

Overnight all flowers blossom;

The next morning fallen petals

are to be swept away.

Change comes with the adjustment of the mind. The presence of worry, anger, anxiety, and other negative thoughts indicates that the mind has reached the point at which something stands in the way and hinders further progress.

The stability that humans seek is only an illusion.

None of us can be happy if nothing ever changes.

True liberation is the ability to remain in a state of complete freedom in the midst of impermanence. It is the ability to live in this changing world from an unchanging oneness of mind and matter. In this state of oneness, we find peace and joy.

Each thought we have presents

an opportunity for change.

Regardless of what the prior thought might have been,

the potential for the next thought is unlimited.

A willingness to embrace

the new and different opens up

opportunities for change.

Impermanence is the display of the unlimited, unceasing, creative power of the Mind. Impermanence is what enables us to change for the better — we can't be better than we already are if everything is fixed permanently.

Thoughts come and go, so how can we

control one thought with another?

The body is impermanent, therefore

how can one body try to relate to another?

Life is inherently unstable unless we find its Source.

Your reality is the result of

ever-changing conditions and karma;

the moment something appears, it also disappears.

This is the nature of existence.

A white egret flies

out of autumn reeds across misty water;

A swallow returns to its dry nest

from a trip in the cold mountains.

A lonely moon shines

brilliantly up in the sky;

Deep into the night

I am sleepless.

造物主

妙柔

4 PHENOMENA

The world, which includes our bodies, thoughts, feelings, perceptions, relationships, and physical environment, is the simultaneously appearing and vanishing display of the formless, boundless Mind. The Mind is not just our psychology; it is the source of life and the Creator of our reality.

The world and all its manifestations

are your creations.

The duality of the observer and the observed is an illusion, because both arise from the Mind. What we see in the world depends on how we see the world. What is good in our lives and what is bad are therefore equally our responsibility.

Each drop of water contains the taste of all water;

every moment contains the essence of all existence.

You are more than the sum

of your thoughts and emotions.

You have potential for unlimited creation and growth,

but you must employ the right tools of the mind.

The reality we face each day is of our own conscious or unconscious making, because we are the sole creator of our life.

Every experience in life is

a reflection of our mind's creation.

Reality does not require our explanation,

nor is our explanation ever reality.

If we hold on to our own definition of reality,

how can reality ever be seen?

Each thought is a universe.

Where the thought is,

life is already unfolding.

Just as the changing color of a single leaf reveals the arrival of autumn, understanding the individual can lead to an understanding of the collective.

Stop seeking the truth outside yourself.

From this moment on, take responsibility

for your own creation.

Thousand-foot waterfall flows into the deep pond;

High waves hit off the bank and splash onto deities.

Behind the water a bird flies back to its nest in a tree;

Unencumbered by the four seasons

the flower of the Self is always in spring.

5 KARMA

Karma is our true legacy; it is the life we create through our thoughts and actions. Karma is the collective whole of our mind's creations. When we blame someone or something for a problem, we try to separate ourselves from our karma. But we will never succeed because the real problem never resides with the other person. The problem has its source in our mind.

The wise man sees when he has been foolish, and learns from it. The foolish man is blind to his folly and refuses to learn.

Karma is simply the reality of this moment.

It is not always negative.

The Buddha has his karma;

each person has his or her own karma too.

When we use our mind improperly, we create karma that leads to suffering. When we use it wisely, however, its infinite creative power becomes the eternal source of happiness and joy, available to us in the here and now.

Every obstacle that manifests in our life is simply a reflection of our inner stagnation.

Face the truth within you

so you can transform your karma.

Intention is like a door within the mind.

With a different type of intention, we can open the door to another realm. With another kind of intention, a distinct karma is created.

Planting the right seed is the only way to guarantee that the right fruit will be harvested.

Take one step at a time as you face your true self.

Do not belittle small good deeds.

The present "you" is the

condensed reflection of the entirety of your life.

The attempt to escape from karma is as futile as trying

to avoid your own shadow under the bright sun.

The present "you" is the only path before you.

When we blame someone or something for a problem,

we are trying to separate ourselves from our karma.

We treat reality as if there were two parts:

One part is us, and the other part is

outside of us, "someone else."

Long and short floral branches

stretch into the spring of March;

Chilly mountain spring flows over boulders.

Everlasting illumination, setting sun glows with red;

There is a master behind the flow of yin and yang

and heaven and earth.

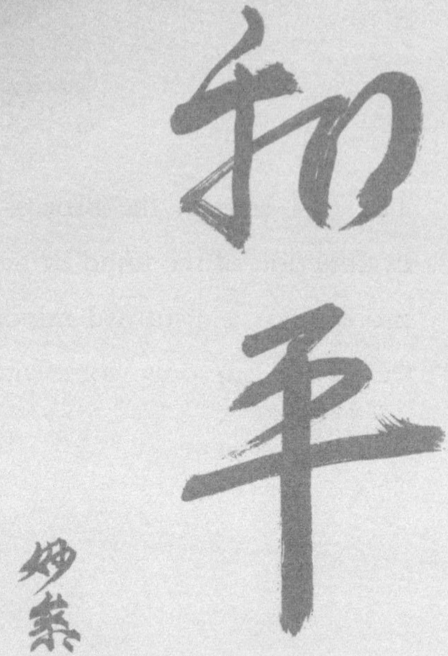
和平

6 A PEACEFUL MIND

The first step in the process of awakening is to stop the dysfunction of the mind by restoring calm. The source of all problems is a disturbed mind; the solution to all problems, therefore, can only come out of that quiet space within your mind.

Remember every step

on your journey toward enlightenment.

The journey, however long it might be,

will reward you with infinite happiness.

A calm mind has the greatest creative potential.

It brings joy that does not depend

on external stimulations.

Every negative emotion and thought

we create is poisonous to our mind and body.

Knowing this, would you take poison little by little?

When a wise person sees a detour sign in life,

he maintains a calm, peaceful mind

and changes his attitude.

A foolish person, however, will only complain.

Anything can be placed on an empty tabletop,

unless you insist that only a certain thing be placed on it.

Similarly, if the mind is free of egotistic concerns,

it can see infinite possibilities.

Put your thoughts away now

so you can experience real life.

Can you release stress without resorting to music, movies, or sensory stimulations of some kind? If so, your mind is less dependent on the environment and knows peace.

You possess limitless potential for creation,

so do not obsess over any particular situation.

If an approach is not working properly, put it aside.

Set a clear goal, and move towards it skillfully,

with a calm mind.

Freedom is not the pursuit of gaining

something; but instead, of letting go.

A mind filled with disturbances cannot be free.

You are usually not aware of ninety-nine percent of your thoughts — but every single one of them has an impact on your life.

The vast sky touches not the earth,

The bright moon illuminates the road Home,

Green are the mountains, white are the reeds —

Thou shall see the Collective for thyself.

淨化

妙宗

7 PURITY

Ego is the beginning of duality: that means separating inside, outside, self, and others. When there is ego, there is a fixed perspective from which we try to do everything. Whether you look up to one person or look down upon another, there is always discrimination. And when you discriminate, you only hurt yourself and obscure the Light within. Spiritual practice is a process of purification whereby all discriminations are set aside.

To perceive the Mind is to

recognize the Creator within yourself.

By accepting reality as it is,

we empower ourselves to make changes

that will lead to a better reality.

Purification is not an outward pursuit but is instead an inner discipline that dissolves our attachments.

Life will be full of contradictions and conflicts until you become the master of your own mind. When that happens, you will be able to have the thoughts you want and release the thoughts you do not want.

You believe you know your self:

your personality, strength, and weaknesses.

But in fact you do not, because with

an impure mind there is no accuracy

in your self-perception.

You must practice inner-reflection —

seeing the darkness and learning to eliminate it

from within — and strive to bring forth

a mind of light, awareness, emptiness, and clarity.

Fundamentally, every person possesses a mind.

This is equality.

Each person's mind can generate thoughts and manifest corresponding phenomena in life.

So again there is equality.

The mind is like water that can either

give a ship buoyancy or sink it.

When we have the ability to generate the thoughts

we desire, we bring forth the life we want.

When we lack mastery over our mind,

we become its victim.

The path to enlightenment lies within, not without.

We must reflect, illuminate, and transform

ourselves from within.

The purpose of Zen practice is

to achieve a pure mind that sees reality as it is,

at ease and free in every moment.

Who is seeing, who is listening, who is talking?

Spring flower, spring breeze, the Spirit's beauty;

Not blind, not deaf, nor speechless,

No eye, no ears, yet wondrous in many ways.

光明之路

8 DEDICATION

As long as our sense of self is built on our thoughts and beliefs, we cannot free ourselves from the problems that result. The quest for selflessness is therefore the practice of freeing the mind from its identification with thoughts and beliefs.

Selflessness is attained when our thoughts and actions are guided by genuine compassion and loving-kindness.

Selflessness is a state of freedom in which we are no longer living life through the duality of "self" and "other." Instead, our life is guided by compassion and loving-kindness for all. This process is simple in concept but not easy in practice; it is a journey of a lifetime.

Though you may not know your true self,

you can always evaluate how your mind works by

looking at the results — are you becoming

more compassionate and wise?

Are your relationships improving?

Religious practice must embody the spirit of equality and universal compassion that embraces all ethnic and cultural differences and allows the beauty of diversity to blossom.

Each thought affects our bodies, our relationships, and our lives, so we should commit our greatest effort to treating everyone around us with loving-kindness, compassion, and equanimity.

The purpose of spiritual practice is to replace our rigid approach to life with gentleness, kindness, and wisdom.

We can easily justify our dislike of another person, but the real question is why does this person appear in our reality in the first place? What is this person reflecting to us about who we are?

How do you bring something new into your life?

You generate thoughts of kindness and compassion

and open your mind to new understanding.

Whether one believes in God, Buddha, or Allah, impermanence remains the truth; the purpose of faith is to elevate the individual within this constantly changing world. We learn to love, to have faith, and to be a better person; and then gradually we are changed for the better.

If you believe the purpose of life is love, then I encourage you to love yourself, your parents, your children, and all the people around you. To do this, you need a pure mind and a kind heart.

In front of the mountain,

the ocean of yellow flowers is colorful.

Behind the hills,

the white silver grass field spans the sky;

Splashing against the rock's crevices,

a place of refuge and rest,

Summoning the wind and rain,

pearly smoke descended.

閑情

妙柔

9 AWAKENING

To awaken to the truth means we live in the truth, which means recognizing that we are the only ones responsible for how we think and act. All of life is contained in this single life moment — the only point of time in which we can decide how to use our mind wisely.

Cause-and-effect is the karmic energy of your existence;

it is a principle to be understood and used.

Awakening is the ultimate gift that anyone can receive,

because it is only through awakening to the truth

that we find fulfillment in life.

First we must acknowledge that we caused all our problems; only then can we find out what erroneous beliefs and thoughts are responsible and practice letting them go.

To change your relationships

and any other conditions in your life,

you must elevate your understanding.

The nature of the Mind is equality —

equality of emptiness, equality of enlightenment,

equality of clarity — because they are universal.

We need to face our flaws with courage and action.

We must use our creative force skillfully in order to

make the necessary changes. By doing so,

we can lead a healthy, vibrant life.

Just as intellectual discussion about food

cannot satisfy hunger,

wisdom cannot come from outside oneself.

The pace of our spiritual maturation

has nothing to do with others.

Every house has its own view

of the bright moon.

The rising fragrance of incense symbolizes elevation.

It reminds us to become more aware and

compassionate with each and every thought.

To elevate your life,

you must look within for answers.

Movement creates shadows;

In quiet the dark mountain's spirit comes alive.

One wise word from the Buddha,

Living utterance that turns stones to gold.

喜悦之心

妙柔

10 PRACTICE

We must never become distracted by the external form of spiritual practice and lose sight of its essence — the manifestation of the Mind's essentially pure, peaceful, awakened nature. To stay on the right course, we must remind ourselves to return constantly to this basic foundation. Each day is a new beginning, when we alone must decide whether to use our mind to elevate our lives or allow our attachments to create more suffering. Life is eternal, so our practice is timeless. Make each moment better than what has been, an attainment made possible because the Mind's creative power never dies.

Everything you need is already in you;

recognize this and practice using your mind correctly.

Complete your practice by bringing the heightened level of awareness into daily life.

Find a suitable practice and transform yourself.

Your practice is your own business, because your thoughts and karma are your own responsibility.

Introspection is not passive as it may appear to be.

In fact, it is very proactive.

When you face yourself, you work directly on

the cause of your problem.

Spiritual cultivation begins

with taming your habitual thoughts.

Be aware of every thought.

Recognize your bad habits and change them

one by one through daily practice.

Reality is often very simple,

but our mind tends to complicate it.

Focus mainly on inner transformations because

they invariably lead to outer improvement.

Growth is always accompanied by

at least a little pain.

Truth in full bloom, arisen in Mind alone,

Moons in a thousand rivers,

Illumined in emptiness-awareness;

Should one inquire into the trifles of worldly affairs,

Seek within yourself, and reap what you sow.

ABOUT THE AUTHOR

Venerable Master Miao Tsan is the author of *Just Use This Mind*, *The Origin Is Pure*, *Intrinsic Awakened Nature*, *Directly Actualize Buddhahood*, *Zen Meditation Guide*, and *Living Truth*, published in Chinese, English, and Spanish. The founder and abbot of Vairocana Zen Monastery in Garden Grove, California, he possesses profound insight into the essence of Zen and has dedicated himself to its propagation and practice. He conducts meditation courses, Zen-Seven and Zen-Three retreats and teaches at universities, medical centers, and television/radio stations in China, Taiwan, Mexico, and the United States. His goal is to open a universal path of wisdom and light by leading people from every tradition toward an understanding of the Truth that transcends time, race, and religion and is without exception.

www.miaotsan.com

Master Your Mind. Master Your Life.